FEB 27 2001

DISCARDED
From the Nashville Public
Library

Property of
Nashville Public Library
615 Church St., Nashville, Tn. 37219

Property of
Nashville Public
Library

READING POWER

High-Tech Vehicles

Supersonic Jets

William Amato

The Rosen Publishing Group's
PowerKids Press™
New York

Published in 2002 by The Rosen Publishing Group, Inc.
29 East 21st Street, New York, NY 10010

Copyright © 2002 by The Rosen Publishing Group, Inc.

All rights reserved. No part of this book may be reproduced in any form without permission in writing from the publisher, except by a reviewer.

First Edition

Book Design: Christopher Logan

Photo Credits: Cover, pp. 6–7 © George Hall/Corbis; pp. 5, 20–21 © U.S. Air Force photo; pp. 8–9, 12–15 © Aero Graphics, Inc./Corbis; p. 11 © Roger Ressmeyer/Corbis; p. 17 © Index Stock Imagery/Walter Geiersperger; pp. 18–19 © Photri Inc.

Amato, William.
Supersonic jets / William Amato.
    p. cm. — (High-tech vehicles)
Includes bibliographical references and index.
ISBN 0-8239-6009-9 (library binding)
1. Supersonic planes—Juvenile literature. 2. Jet planes,
Military—Juvenile literature. 3. Concorde (Jet transports)—Juvenile
literature. I. Title.
TL551.5 .A43 2001
629.132'305—dc21

                                                    2001000275

Manufactured in the United States of America

Contents

Supersonic Jets

Supersonic jets are the fastest airplanes in the world. They fly more than twice as fast as other jets. Most supersonic jets are used by the military.

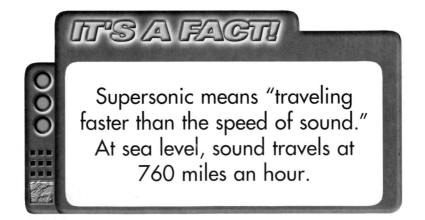

IT'S A FACT!

Supersonic means "traveling faster than the speed of sound." At sea level, sound travels at 760 miles an hour.

Building Supersonic Jets

Supersonic jets are thin and pointed. This shape helps them fly fast through the air.

Supersonic jets have big engines. The engines push air out of the tail pipes. This moves the plane forward.

Types of Supersonic Jets

Most fighter jets can fly at supersonic speeds. Fighter jets are small planes that have short, thin wings. The wings help the pilot turn the plane quickly.

The Blue Angels flying team is part of the U.S. Navy.

This is the B-1B *Lancer*. It is a long-range bomber. This supersonic jet can fly long distances without having to stop for fuel.

The B-1B bomber uses equipment that stops enemy radar from working well.

IT'S A FACT!

Radar sends out radio waves to find planes. Radio waves bounce off planes and the planes show up on radar screens.

This kind of plane is the only supersonic passenger jet. It carries people from city to city. It flies between the United States and Europe.

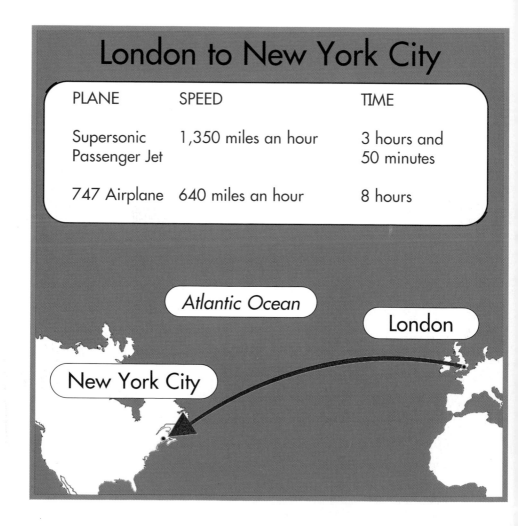

London to New York City

PLANE	SPEED	TIME
Supersonic Passenger Jet	1,350 miles an hour	3 hours and 50 minutes
747 Airplane	640 miles an hour	8 hours

Atlantic Ocean

London

New York City

The wings of the supersonic passenger jet are shaped like a triangle. They help the jet to fly at supersonic speeds.

IT'S A FACT!

The fuel for this plane is stored in its wings.

Future Flights

Supersonic jets have changed the world we live in. They make traveling faster. Supersonic jets play an important part in our world.

Glossary

long-range (**lawng-raynj**) able to travel long distances

military (**mihl**-uh-tehr-ee) men and women working in the armed forces

radar (**ray**-dahr) a machine that uses radio waves to find planes in the sky

supersonic jets (**soo**-puhr-**sahn**-ihk **jehts**) planes that fly more than 760 miles an hour.

Resources

Books

Jet Fighter: The Harrier AV-8B
by Julie Beyer
Children's Press (2000)

Supersonic Fighters: The F-16 Fighting Falcons
by Bill Sweetman
Capstone Press (2001)

Web Site

Supersonic Spies
http://www.pbs.org/wgbh/nova/supersonic/

Index

Word Count: 241

Note to Librarians, Teachers, and Parents

If reading is a challenge, Reading Power is a solution! Reading Power is perfect for readers who want high-interest subject matter at an accessible reading level. These fact-filled, photo-illustrated books are designed for readers who want straightforward vocabulary, engaging topics, and a manageable reading experience. With clear picture/text correspondence, leveled Reading Power books put the reader in charge. Now readers have the power to get the information they want and the skills they need in a user-friendly format.